D1006471

THE NATURE

海

OF THE

松

CHINESE

林

CHARACTER

Text by Barbara Aria
Calligraphy by Russell Eng Gon
吴文忠
Illustrations by Lesley Ehlers

Simon and Schuster
New York London Toronto Sydney Tokyo Singapore

A RUNNING HEADS BOOK

Simon and Schuster
Simon & Schuster Building
Rockefeller Center
1230 Avenue of the Americas
New York, New York 10020

SIMON AND SCHUSTER and colophon are registered trademarks
of Simon & Schuster Inc.

THE NATURE OF THE CHINESE CHARACTER
was conceived and produced by
Running Heads Incorporated
55 West 21 Street
New York, New York 10010

Editor: Charles A. de Kay
Designer: Lesley Ehlers
Consulting Editor: Russell Eng Gon
Managing Editor: Lindsey Crittenden
Production Manager: Linda Winters

1 3 5 7 9 10 8 6 4 2

Library of Congress Cataloging in Publication Data

Aria, Barbara.
The nature of the Chinese character / by Barbara Aria;
calligraphy by Russell Eng Gon ; illustrations by Lesley Ehlers.
p. cm.
ISBN 0-671-72886-5
1. Chinese language—Writing. 2. Chinese language—Etymology.
3. Calligraphy, Chinese. I. Gon, Russell Eng. II. Ehlers, Lesley.
III. Title.
PL1171.A75 1991

495.1′11—dc20 90-45291
CIP

Typeset by Crane Typesetting Service, Inc.
Color Separations by Hong Kong Scanner Craft Company, Ltd.
Printed and bound in Singapore by Times Offset Pte. Ltd.

To my mother

Acknowledgments

Many people were involved in the making of this book. To begin at the beginning, I should like to thank Marta Hallett of Running Heads Incorporated, who conceived and developed this project, and Caroline Herter and Patricia Leasure of Simon and Schuster, who supported it. My thanks also to everybody at Running Heads who helped bring this book to completion, especially to Charles de Kay, my editor. Special thanks to Russell Gon, with whom it was my pleasure to collaborate, and to Lesley Ehlers who designed and illustrated the book.

Contents

Introduction

Long, long ago, after the time of the tree-nesting people, after the discovery of fire, after the time of the drilling men, in the hundred-year reign of the Yellow Emperor Huang-Ti when civilization was born, there lived a man named Tsang Chieh, official recorder to Huang-Ti.

At night, hearing the ghosts wail for the creation of writing, Tsang Chieh looked up with his four eyes at the pointed rays of the star Wen Ch'ang, Lord of Literature. Inspired, Tsang Chieh looked down to see the footprints of the birds and animals. He watched the shadows cast by trees and vegetation. He saw the patterns of tortoise shell markings. Observing the forms of nature, Tsang Chieh copied them by scratching onto sticks of smoothed bamboo. These were the first Chinese pictograms.

So goes the legend, recorded by the historian Chang Yen-Yuan in the year A.D. 847. By Chang Yen-Yuan's time, in the T'ang dynasty, the modern calligraphic script of China had been established and systematized, and the printing of books had begun. Chinese civilization was already reaching its peak, in part owing to a system of writing that not only united the country's diverse regions, but also provided some continuity from the administrative rule of one dynasty to the next.

Chang Yen-Yuan placed the legendary invention of Chinese writing in the twenty-eighth century B.C.—a time of great cultural development in China and the dawn of Chinese history. Whatever truth is to be found in the legend of Tsang Chieh, it is believed that the first Chinese characters were indeed invented early in the second millennium B.C., and it is clear that their invention was based on observations of nature.

Initially, writing was used by the ruling dynasty in connection with the ritual consultation of "oracle bones." Tortoise shells and the shoulder blades of animals were engraved with written characters and were then treated with a heated bronze pin, producing cracks on the reverse side of the bones or shells. The direction and length of the cracks in relation to the characters were interpreted as signs determining important decisions of state—among them, the correct times for planting and harvesting crops.

Ritual arts, such as the reading of oracle bones, were highly valued in ancient China; they could make the difference between a fruitful or a poor harvest. Intricately connected with these rituals, calligraphy was elevated to one of the most treasured of Chinese arts, and it remains so to this day. Calligraphy is considered one of the highest art forms, along with painting and drawing. All three are linked by the brush that creates them and by the world of natural forms that inspires them. In China, writing, as much as painting or drawing, is practiced, collected, preserved, and valued as an art form. In many houses, strips of paper or silk bearing graceful calligraphy decorate the walls; whether they are mass-produced pieces or priceless original works, these calligraphic decorations are often given pride of place.

Perhaps more than any art, writing has held a special, almost sacred place in Chinese culture. Traditionally, any piece of paper with writing on it was esteemed so highly that it was considered disrespectful to simply throw it away; instead, waste paper with writing was routinely taken for burning to a special Pagoda of Compassionating the Characters. Although this practice died out during this century, the calligraphic character still commands respect. During the ascendancy of Mao Tse-tung, for instance, examples of the leader's calligraphy were reproduced and widely distributed among the general population, to be admired, cherished, and preserved.

For centuries, knowledge of written characters was the carefully guarded privilege of the nobility and their servants. But, with the spread of literacy, the art of calligraphy has become a popular pastime of the people. The Chinese character connects the China of today with its own distant past. Chinese is unique among the languages of the world in that it has changed little over the centuries; texts written three thousand years ago can still be read and understood today, and the sprawling characters emblazoned by students on long red banners between bamboo poles at Tiananmen Square in the spring of 1989 were essentially the same as those once scratched on bones in the dawn of China's history.

In the words of Chang Yen-Yuan, "Writing grew from the need to express ideas. . . . This was the intention and purpose of nature and of the sages." The first characters were very much like primitive pictures representing those things that were necessary for the divination of oracles and for day-to-day transactions in a simple culture: the animals owned or hunted; the protection of territory; the weather; the body; the land; the family.

The earliest examples of a Chinese written "script" were found around the turn of this century, engraved on oracle bones dating from the Shang-Yin dynasty, eighteenth century B.C. These primitive characters are known as "Shell-and-Bone" script. Over time, they were refined and formalized; characters found inscribed on bronze and stone tablets (known as "Small Seal" script) dating from the first millennium B.C. were already somewhat abstracted from their earlier, pictorial forms. The materials and techniques used also shaped the evolution of the characters—from bones and shells to metals, stone, silk, and paper; from scratching to brushwork. And, as Chinese society grew more complex, new characters were invented. By around A.D. 200 a list of over ten thousand characters existed, and the first Chinese etymological dictionary, *Hiu Shen*, had been written.

This dictionary shows how character construction developed, as the demand for new words grew. Obviously, not every object, act, or concept could be simply translated into a pictogram; other ways had to be found of expressing words in such a way that they could be easily understood.

Hiu Shen listed four broad, graphic principles for character construction. First came the simple pictograms, derived from Shell-and-Bone characters, and known as "imitating the form." The character for 'tree', for example, shows a stylized trunk, roots, and branches. Some pictograms were given several meanings; the character for 'elephant', for instance, also means 'to make' or 'to shape', in reference to the carving of ivory.

Sometimes simple pictograms were doubled or tripled, or modified with an additional stroke to form a new meaning; three 'trees' standing together came to mean 'dense', or 'thick'; by adding a line through the base of the trunk, the character for 'tree' was modified to mean 'root' (today, the original meaning has been lost and that character simply means 'origin' or 'source'). Characters such as these are known as simple ideograms, or "pointing at the thing," since they portray ideas through metaphors with natural objects.

But the Chinese universe was expanding rapidly, and human affairs were growing increasingly more sophisticated. Cities had to be built, goods traded, wars fought, fields divided into plots to be ploughed, tilled, and planted. Meanwhile, monks and scholars were developing complex philosophical systems that required a vastly expanded written vocabulary. The *I-Ching,* or *Book of Changes,* still one of the most widely studied of ancient Chinese texts, was first put to paper in the Chou dynasty, about three thousand years ago. How was the Chinese character script extended to the point where such an intricate cosmological system as the *I-Ching* could be expressed?

A large number of new words became possible by "joining the meanings" of words in composite ideograms. Here, two or more pictograms were combined to form a new character through association, or metaphor. The character for 'to love', for instance, was formed by joining 'woman' and 'child'; 'to speak' is a 'word' in a 'mouth'. By adding on pictograms, a wide range of words becomes possible; 'to speak' with a 'pen' makes a 'book'.

Although in present-day Chinese life people tend not to be conscious of the joining of ideas as they write—just as we say the words 'road' and 'ride', for example, without recognizing their connection—these characters contain a latent poetry and provide many clues about ancient Chinese culture and thought. The character for 'precious', for example, shows an emblematic rooftop, sheltering gold, earthenware, and a cowrie shell (early Chinese currency). The character for 'old' shows the characters for 'ten' over 'mouth'—as old as ten mouths, or generations.

Far less poetic, but more predominant, were characters formed by "harmonizing the sound." Here, two or more characters were joined in such a way that one part, known as the *radical,* suggested the general meaning of the word, while the other part, the *phonetic,* indicated the sound. These are known as composite phonograms.

There are many words in Chinese that sound the same, but mean different things (known as homophones, like the words *wear* and *ware* in English). In spoken Chinese, homophones are differentiated through subtle inflections in pronunciation. In the written language, however, it is through the radical that one determines meaning. For example, the Chinese words for 'mother' and 'horse' are homophones; they are both pronounced *ma*, although they are written differently. The character for mother borrows the pictogram for 'horse', telling us what the sound of the word is, and combines it with the character for 'woman', indicating the meaning of the word. Phonograms such as these make up about three quarters of all Chinese characters.

Phonograms were developed relatively late in the evolution of Chinese script. By then, many words associated with the most basic aspects of day-to-day life were already in existence. And since daily life in ancient China, as in any traditional culture, was intricately connected to the natural world of mountains and rivers, sun and moon, animals and vegetation, many words that signify aspects of nature date back to the first days of writing, when characters were formed pictorially or by combining ideas, rather than phonetically. Thus, any collection of characters representing things in nature is bound to contain more than its share of poetry and visual charm.

The contemplation of nature, as an aesthetic and spiritual experience, has always been central to the lives of Chinese artists, scholars, and monks. While Western painters perfected the art of portraiture, the artists of China devoted themselves to landscape painting. Where figures exist in these paintings, they are nearly always tiny parts of nature, dwarfed by the vast expanses of land that stretch, rise, and flow around them.

Chinese poets, too, have celebrated the beauty of nature's ways—of waterfalls rushing against the massive stillness of a mountain; of mists swirling around its peak; of the turning of leaves; or of horses galloping riderless across a plain. Nature is not seen as something to be mastered by man. It is what it is, a fact; the Chinese term for nature means "self-thus." By observing it, man can gain insights into his own life and that of his society.

In Chinese thought, nature is seen as constantly in flux. It represents in large and small ways the eternally repeating life cycle of which mankind is also a part. The life of the universe and the patterns of human affairs are inseparable, and the ultimate goal of the arts, including calligraphy, is to express their coherence.

Just as all things originally came from one, so artistic creation has its origin in the first stroke ever made, and each character or painting begins with one brush stroke whose nature determines the ones that follow. The outer, visible form of the character, like the outer form of bamboo or tiger, reveals its inner life. The beauty of a Chinese character, therefore, can have the same effect on the mind and heart as the beauty of nature. And nature provides the inspiration.

Since the natural universe and the world of humans mirror each other, nature becomes a metaphor for human affairs. A great number of Chinese sayings are based on this—even political slogans, such as Mao's allusion to the unity of the army and the people: "as close as fish and water." Many combined-idea characters are formed in the same way, through metaphor with nature. The character for 'east', for example, shows the sun in the branches of a tree—the sun rising. The water radical itself—the graphic core of the character for 'water'—is found in a huge number of compound ideograms.

The written language of China is rich in nature images, and the strokes themselves suggest the natural forms of the universe. They should move, like living things, just as a living piece of grass bends and a petal curls. The stroke grows as it is made, becoming in that instant a thing that is in spirit like the mountain or the stream. Once executed, it is what it is. No corrections are made.

There are seven standardized types of stroke, referred to as the "Seven Mysteries." Each, when ideally executed, is identified with a natural form; for instance, a horizontal stroke should be like a cloud that slowly drifts across the sky; a dot should take its form from that of a falling rock; a vertical stroke should seem like an ancient but strong vine stem. Other types of stroke and dot have been likened to a sheep's leg, a tiger's claw, an apricot kernel, a dewdrop, a new moon, and a wave rising and falling.

Each type of stroke is made with a particular movement of the hand and arm, and in every character a specific sequence of strokes is to be followed. (This sequence is one of the first things one learns in making characters.) If the strokes are executed in the wrong order, or if the brush travels in the wrong direction, the character looks wrong. In other words, the rhythm that one sees in a Chinese character—in the flow of its strokes, the thickness and thinness of its lines, the relationship between its dots—is the visual embodiment of the rhythm of the writer's hand as it moves the brush, up and down, side to side. The quality of movement, as in nature, is all important.

This rhythm does not come easily. It requires a skill gained through incessant practice, a calmness of spirit, and the right materials. Chinese schoolchildren begin a systematic training in calligraphy from around the age of seven, by tracing over characters. They learn how to hold the brush very tightly, and how to grind the ink so that there is the correct balance of water and pigment. If the balance is too watery, the "flesh" of the stroke will be loose; if the ink is too thick, the flesh will be fat.

Students learn how to fill an imaginary square with each character, so that the composition looks natural and pleasing to the eye. The strokes within each character, and even between characters, should seem to be joined by "muscles."

The strength of the writer's hand gives a stroke its "bone." If the flesh of the writing is fat but it has no bones, the calligraphy is deemed "piggy." Students are therefore taught, in making strokes, how to best position the body, and how to raise the wrist and elbow so that they are held level with each other, the wrist and brush held almost perpendicular to the paper. The ideal position of the calligrapher's arm has been compared to the outstretched leg of a crane. In Chinese calligraphy, many of the keys to technique are found in nature.

Only after the examples of the masters have been faithfully copied, over and over, does the serious student of calligraphy begin to develop a personal style, and here again the world of nature often provides the inspiration. It is said that the monk Huai-Su refined his personal style after watching clouds drift through the summer sky. Many great calligraphers of the past retreated to the hills or forests in order to observe nature and attain a state of inner tranquillity. Today, students of calligraphy are advised to practice in the early morning, when mind and world are calm, and the light of the sun is at its clearest.

The Nature of the Chinese Character is an evocation of the natural world, as China has seen and written it. Forty characters, rendered by brush in the contemporary or "regular" style, are each accompanied by an explanation of the character's construction and evolution, and an illustration representing the word pictorially. Where a character has evolved graphically over time and its evolution is known, evolutionary stages are shown beside the character itself. And for anyone who seeks not only to appreciate the beauty of the characters and the poetry inherent in their construction, but also to find enjoyment in their making, the stroke order for each character is given on the page facing the character. After all, each person, like each character, must begin with the first stroke; and then, as the Chinese proverb says, "Good practice can produce skillfulness." The true art of the Chinese character is a lifelong pursuit. This book offers a brief introduction and a glimpse of a rich and fascinating universe.

土

一
十
土

The earth, *t'u*, encompasses all of nature. Yet it is represented in the most minimal form in this abstract ideogram containing the character for 'ten', which in Chinese also means 'complete': earth as the complete body. A simple baseline denotes 'earth', below, just as 'sky' is defined by the line above.

In Chinese thought, the form of our earth is brought to maturity by man, through the creation of cities. And so, by adding 'grown-up' to the character for 'earth', we have 'city': the earth, in its natural completeness, developed by man.

Earth t'u

風

Wind feng

Wind, like earth and sky, is one of the primal forces of nature. It is timeless, unceasing, yet in time it brings about change in the skies above, and by extension, on the earth below: the wind brings rain, then scatters clouds to reveal the warming sun.

In Chinese thought, the world of nature and the world of man are linked, reflecting each other in ways large and small. And so in Chinese, *feng* also means 'breath', the wind we breathe.

The precise origins of this character are lost in time. It seems, however, to contain elements from two words—'phoenix' or 'sail', both of which suggest movement through space; and a modification of the radical for 'reptile' or 'insect', denoting change.

火

A primal force in nature, fire darts upward, its flames clinging to each other as do the strokes in this simple pictogram.

Man's first use of fire was in China, about 600,000 B.C. According to the *Pai Hu T'ung*, written in the first century A.D., the mythical founder of civilization observed the world of nature and the forces that regulate all things, including fire, and proceeded to invent the idea of cooking. Today, the Chinese characters for 'fry', 'braise', and 'boil', retain their link with fire.

Fire huo

湖

Lake hu

The character for 'lake', or "a sheet of water," is something of a riddle. Comprising three elements, its meaning is determined by the radical, three interrelated strokes suggesting drops of liquid. Combined with this are the characters for 'moon' and 'old', or 'long life'.

Only in lakes does water rest. Bounded by land on all sides, it lies perfectly still, reflective. Unlike flowing water, which is eternally young, the water of the lake does not flow infinitely through space. It is old water. And in the long-lived waters of the lake, shines the moon.

江

Any character containing the 'water' radical has some association with water. 'Mist', 'steam', 'soup', have 'water' as their determining characteristic. The qualities of water are expressed in 'vast' and 'eternal', which also contain the radical. To differentiate one word from another, it is combined with one or more characters to create a separate, often metaphoric meaning.

Many of these "combined idea" words, developed thousands of years ago, still retain hints of traditional thought and culture. Here, the three short strokes signifying drops of water are combined with the character for 'work', acknowledging the importance of rivers for irrigation and for transporting goods and people across the vast terrains of China.

River chiang

山

山

A mountain soars upward and sinks downward; like water, it expresses motion, although it is forever still and has an unchanging inner nature. Each rise is connected to a fall, like night and day. "The mountains pile up on one another, break off into ravines and deep valleys in the most unexpected zigzag manner," wrote the seventeenth-century artist-monk Shih-t'ao.

The character for 'mountain', or 'hills', is a simple pictogram depicting three hills. In its original form, resembling the three peaks of a crown, this pictogram has been found carved on bones and shells dating from the Shang dynasty, around 1700 to 1100 B.C.

Mountain shan

波

Water has depth, and it has surface. The lake's surface is like a sheet, while the surface of the sea surges in waves—vibrating particles of liquid responding to natural forces.

The character for 'waves', or 'breakers', made up of the 'water' radical combined with *pi*, meaning 'skin' or 'covering', reflects a universal phenomenon—waves move across the surface of the sea's water, not beneath it.

Waves: the skin of the water.

Waves po

貝

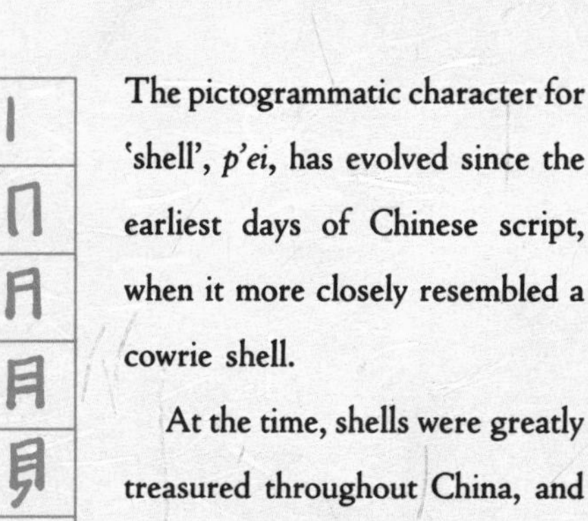

The pictogrammatic character for 'shell', *p'ei*, has evolved since the earliest days of Chinese script, when it more closely resembled a cowrie shell.

At the time, shells were greatly treasured throughout China, and by 1000 B.C. were used as currency in the marketplace. Therefore, this character also means 'valuable'. When 'shell' or 'valuable' was combined with the character for 'net', a new word, 'to buy', was made. The character for 'shell' remains central to the world of commerce in modern-day China.

Shell p'ei

Many ancient pictograms have, in the course of time, lost some of their pictorial qualities. A few have evolved so far from their origins that they now resemble characters to which they are, in fact, completely unrelated.

Yü, the character for 'fish', started life as a simple image showing head, tail, and fins. Many hundreds of years later the fish is barely recognizable—in its place we have instead something that resembles a combination of two characters, 'field' and 'fire'. By coincidence, then, *yü* offers us a wonderfully startling image of the fish swimming in a field of water, its silvery skin flashing like fire in the sunlight.

Fish yü

鶴

Crane ho

Among the many symbols of success and longevity in Chinese culture is the crane, represented in this ideogram by a pair of 'bird' pictograms, one of which has a 'roof' over its head.

People all over the world have invested the crane with special meanings, particularly the ability to bring good fortune. In China, the bird is noted for the tender way in which it cares for its young, and for its old and infirm parents; standing together, cranes protect each other in the interest of long life. Because the crane returns to the same nesting place year after year, it has a 'roof'.

Crane: the homing bird that stands in pairs.

The beautiful and familiar image of a swan floating gracefully on the water is suggested in this character, which combines 'bird' with the character for 'river'. But when the swan spreads its wings and soars skyward one is struck suddenly by its immensity. And so *hung*—'swan' or 'river bird'—has come to mean also 'vast'.

Interestingly, this word is almost interchangeable with another Chinese word for 'vast' or 'profound', also pronounced *hung*, which joins the characters for 'water' and 'united' to denote 'a flood of ideas'!

Swan hung

鴨

Like many Chinese characters for animals, the duck is defined by its observable qualities. The pictogram for 'long-tailed bird' is used as a determinate, while next to it the character for 'armor' or 'protective covering' signifies the type of bird.

Ducks are among the hardiest of animals, weathering alike the fierce heat of summer and the harsh days of winter, when lakes and rivers turn to ice. For this reason the duck is known as "the bird protected as if by armor."

Duck ya

田

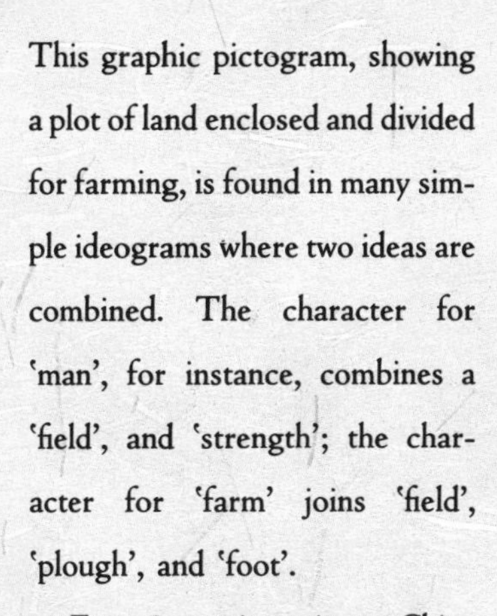

This graphic pictogram, showing a plot of land enclosed and divided for farming, is found in many simple ideograms where two ideas are combined. The character for 'man', for instance, combines a 'field', and 'strength'; the character for 'farm' joins 'field', 'plough', and 'foot'.

Even in ancient times, China had a well-developed system of subsistence agriculture. There is evidence that the people of southern China were clearing forest to make fields as far back as 10,000 B.C. According to legend it was Shen Nung, the Divine Husbandman, who split a piece of wood for a plowshare, bent a piece of wood for the handle, and taught the art of tilling the fields.

Field t'ian

苗

In the character for 'sprout' we see an agricultural 'field' combined with the four vibrant strokes of the 'grass' radical: sprout, the cultivated grass.

"When a young bamboo sprouts, it is only an inch long, but the joints and leaves are already latent in it," wrote a Chinese painter of the eleventh century A.D. The sprouting of seeds evokes the promise of the future, and the abundance of nature as tended by man.

Nearly every traditional culture has made a connection between its children and its crops. In China, this link is expressed in the language itself; the word for 'sprout', *miao*, also means 'progeny' or 'offspring'.

Sprout miao

花

Hidden at first among the leaves of a plant, buds slowly unfold to become fully opened flowers. In the Chinese character for 'flower', the 'grass' radical is qualified by the character 'change', or 'metamorphosis': flower, the grass transformed.

The character for 'change' shown here is said to have been originally formed by the image of a man tumbling head over heels. But change was not always so closely associated with flowers; in the ancient form of the character *hua*, the flowering quality of the plant was expressed simply by the addition of more grass.

Flower hua

園

The Chinese character for 'garden' or 'orchard' looks deceptively like a pictogram, with garden walls surrounding plants and trees. In fact, it is a rich and complex ideogram combining the characters for 'earth', 'mouth', and 'cloth' within a square that represents 'enclosure'—'earth', the bed of life; 'mouth', telling us that life is there for the eating; 'cloth', giving the idea of something spread out.

The garden: a place where the earth is covered with the food of life, as if spread over with a cloth.

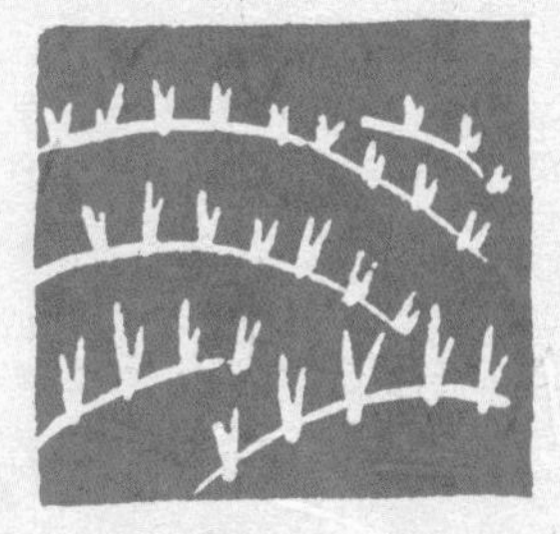

Garden yuan

竹

"Bamboo without mind, yet it sends thoughts soaring to the clouds," wrote the fourteenth-century poet Wu Chen.

Represented by one of the purest of Chinese pictograms, bamboo is, by tradition, central to the culture and art of China. The firm stalk and yielding leaves expressed in the character help the plant to survive the rays of the sun and the weight of the snow; in fact, bamboo only grows stronger as it adapts to environmental conditions. For the Chinese it therefore symbolizes the qualities of enlightenment—strength and adaptiveness.

Bamboo chu

一 十 才 木

'Trees' and the 'wood' they give us are interchangeable in the Chinese language; the same word, *mu*, is used for both. It is expressed in writing by a simple pictogram showing the upright trunk intersected by a line representing branches, with the roots below.

Many Chinese characters are based on the 'tree' pictogram. The trunk alone denotes the word 'counting'; in ancient China, stems were commonly used for this purpose. Adding a line through the base and roots of the tree denotes 'root' in the sense of 'origin'. The Chinese ideograms for 'carpenter', 'plank', and 'clogs' also contain the 'tree' pictogram, as does the word for 'numb'; the Chinese often refer to a person who is without feeling, or emotionally numb, as 'wooden'.

Tree mu

林

A multiplicity of trees, represented in this character by two 'trees' side by side, makes *lin*, a 'forest' or 'grove'—a graphic and simple ideogram formed by doubling the pictogram.

Adding a third 'tree', nestled between and above the first two, makes a luxuriant forest. This is the character *sen*, which has also come to mean 'dense' or 'dark', as in a forest thick with trees.

Forest lin

The tree develops slowly, almost imperceptibly; its changing qualities are most readily expressed through its leaves, in which both the cycle of the seasons and the successive change of generations are so clearly manifested.

The Chinese character for 'leaf', *yeh*, emphasizes this essential quality of change that unites the organic and the human worlds; 'tree' at the bottom and the 'grass' radical at the top are joined by the character for 'generations'.

Leaf: the seasonal life and death of the tree.

Leaf yeh

蝶

The Chinese character for 'butterfly' is a composite ideogram made up of three elements: 'leaf', 'generations', and the 'worm' radical that occurs in most characters for reptilian life, including insects.

The butterfly and the leaf are connected in more than one way. Whether fluttering or tentatively still, the leaf and the wings of a butterfly resemble one another in their delicate movement and posture. And the life cycle of the butterfly, like that of the leaf, provides us with a focus for the contemplation of generational change.

Butterfly tieh

菜

The 'grass' radical is used to suggest all kinds of vegetation, including, of course, vegetables. Here, we see the radical joined with the characters for 'tree' (at the bottom) and 'claw' (the four fingerlike strokes in the middle) —two characters which in themselves combine in meaning to form 'to pick' or 'to pluck'. A vegetable, therefore, is grass that one picks with one's hands.

This all-purpose character—when modified by other words—provides us with a wide assortment of vegetables. Perhaps the best known is a variety of Chinese cabbage called bok choy *(pei ts'ai)*, the 'white vegetable'.

Vegetable ts'ai

種

種

The Chinese character for 'grain' or 'seed' shows a modified 'tree' bending over at the top, combined with the character for 'something heavy' or 'weighty'.

This ideogram tells us two things about grain: it suggests the nodding heads of slender millet or corn stems, as their clusters of seed ripen and grow heavy; and it tells us that, for the farmer who has tended his crops, it is the grain itself that counts as the most significant, or 'weighty', part of the plant.

Grain chung

秋
秋
秋

秋

The Chinese ideogram for 'autumn' joins the characters for 'crops' and 'fire' in a striking image for this important season in the yearly cycle—a season that traditionally ends with the burning of the grain stubble in the fields, enriching the soil for the next year's crops.

Autumn ch'iu

The character for 'crops', a modification of 'tree', shows how the weight of grain that is ripe for harvesting makes the plant bend at the top. But this character conjures up other autumnal images, too: the fiery colors of fall foliage, and the activity that goes into the harvesting of crops.

Autumn: when nature is all ablaze.

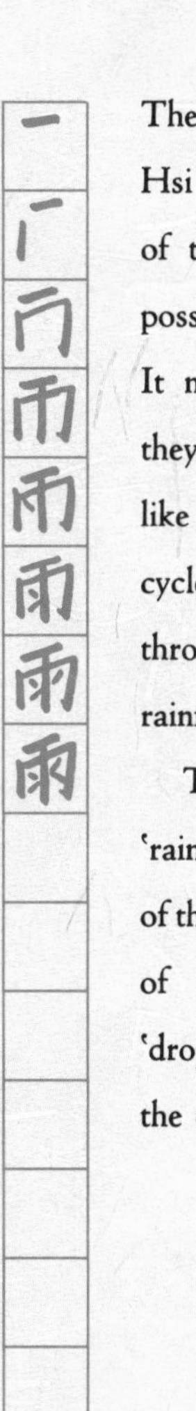

The eleventh-century painter Kuo Hsi spoke of water as "the blood of the universe." Water makes possible the life cycles of nature. It nourishes the crops, so that they germinate and sprout. And, like all of nature, water follows a cycle of its own, expressed through evaporation upward and rainfall downward.

The Chinese character for 'rain' emphasizes the cyclic nature of this process by joining an image of water, suggested by four 'drops' falling from the sky, with the character for 'cycle'.

Rain yü

雲
雲
雲
雲
雲

Combined with ‘speak’, rain becomes ‘cloud’; in traditional Chinese thought, clouds do not so much obscure the sun as speak of the rain that is so essential to life.

The Chinese language contains many different words to describe various kinds of cloud—names like ‘rosy clouds’, ‘white clouds’, and ‘passing clouds’, that capture the shapes, colors, and movement of clouds as they appear in the sky. Since clouds tend to appear in flocks, the character *yün* also means ‘numerous’ and ‘to gather’.

Cloud *yün*

'Clouds' over the 'fields' mean 'thunder', described in the *I-Ching* as "the invisible sound that moves all hearts" and "awakens the seeds."

Thunder is the mysterious voice that precedes an electrical storm, when rainclouds burst over the fields; thus, the Chinese say, thunder in a drought makes the peasants happy.

Thunder can also have ominous overtones, however; the ideogram *lei* has been borrowed as a component in the characters for violent rages and for tools of war such as torpedoes.

Thunder lei

日
日

The character for 'sun' has evolved into a highly stylized pictogram since ancient days. First scratched onto oracle bones during the second millennium B.C., the bright center of the sun was a dot within the circle of its rays.

A few hundred years later, as the character *jih* was inscribed on bronze and stone, the dot became a line and the circle began to lose its contours. By the time the modern style was established about fourteen hundred years ago, paper and ink were in use; the bright center of the sun was now a line within the square of its rays.

Sun jih

星

The character for 'star', *hsing*, means also 'point of light', 'spark'. It is formed by combining the pictogram 'sun' with the character for 'to be born'.

Perhaps the ancient Chinese thought that the sparkling points of light they observed in the night sky were like tiny, newborn suns. Certainly, observation of the stars' movements helped them to determine times of planting and harvesting crops.

Star hsing

春

Spring ch'un

As the morning follows the night, spring follows winter, the stern season when snow and ice cover the ground and the immense northern regions of China grow bare and windblown.

Spring brings the melting of the ice and the warming of the earth. Seeds germinate, giving new life to the world. All this is the work of the sun, which seems to fill the spring sky with new hope. Therefore, the Chinese character for 'spring' shows the 'sun', *jih*, joined with an exaggeratedly 'big' pictogram: spring, season of the great sun.

月
月
月

Like the pictogram 'sun', the Chinese character for 'moon' and 'lunar month' has changed considerably from its earliest known form—the crescent moon of oracle bone script. By the fifth century B.C., astrological science in China was capable of predicting a lunar eclipse, although the science later fell into decline.

'Sun' and 'moon' together form the character for 'bright', *ming*, which in the fourteenth century gave its name to the Ming dynasty, a time of great cultural flowering.

Moon yueh

龍